How flowers grow

Emma Helbrough
Designed by Catherine-Anne MacKinnon
and Laura Parker

Illustrated by Maggie Silver and Uwe Mayer

Flower consultant: Dr. Margaret Rostron

Reading consultant: Alison Kelly,
Roehampton University

Contents

3 Lots of flowers

4 Seeds to seedlings

6 Plant parts

8 Making food

10 Buds to flowers

12 Pollen and nectar

14 Making seeds

16 Spreading seeds

18 Juicy fruit

20 New plants

22 Rainforest flowers

24 Hot deserts

26 Water plants

28 Killer plants

30 Glossary of flower words

31 Web sites to visit

32 Index

Lots of flowers

There are thousands of different kinds of flowers growing all over the world.

These amazing flowers are passion flowers.

Seeds to seedlings

A seed has a hard shell with a young plant inside. Seeds grow in the soil when the sun and rain has made them warm and wet.

These are sunflower seeds.

Each sunflower seed can grow into a big sunflower.

In the soil, the shell of a seed splits.

A small root sprouts out of it.

Then a shoot grows out of the seed.

When a shoot breaks through the soil, it is called a seedling.

The largest seed in the world is the coco de mer. It is bigger than a football.

Plant parts

Most plants are made up of flowers, leaves, roots and stems.

This is a wood sorrel plant.

The stems keep the plant upright. Leaves and flowers grow on the stems.

Plants make food in their green leaves.

Some plants have leaves that are sharp and spiky.

They grow well as animals prefer to eat smooth leaves.

Lots of things you eat are plant parts. Broccoli is a bunch of flowers and carrots are a kind of root.

Underground, the roots soak up water from the soil. They hold the plant in place too.

Making food

Plants need food to grow. They use sunlight, air and water to make their food.

The leaves soak up air and sunlight.

Then the leaves suck rainwater up the stem from the roots.

The water, sunlight and air make food in the leaves.

Hyacinth   Tulip   Bluebell   Amaryllis

Some plants store their food in bulbs, which are made up of layers of special leaves.

Onions are a type of bulb. If you cut one in half, you can see its layers.

Buds to flowers

When a seedling has grown into a strong plant, it is ready to grow flowers.

Baby flowers are called buds.

The petals are tightly packed inside a bud.

Slowly a bud begins to open.

Its petals start to appear.

The petals open into a flower.

Stamen

In the middle of a flower there are long tubes called stamens.

On the tips of the stamens there is some powder called pollen. Plants use pollen to make seeds.

Edelweiss flowers grow in cold places. They have a fluffy coat of hairs to keep them warm.

Pollen and nectar

Inside a flower there is a sweet juice called nectar. As insects and birds drink nectar, they take pollen from one flower to another.

When a bee drinks nectar, pollen sticks to its furry body.

It flies to another flower of the same kind and some of the pollen drops off.

This flower now has some pollen from another flower.

Pollen can rub onto a hummingbird's beak as it drinks nectar.

The pollen rubs off onto the next flower that the hummingbird visits.

Bees can collect nectar from over 1,000 flowers before they feel full!

Making seeds

Plants start to grow seeds as soon as they have some pollen from another plant.

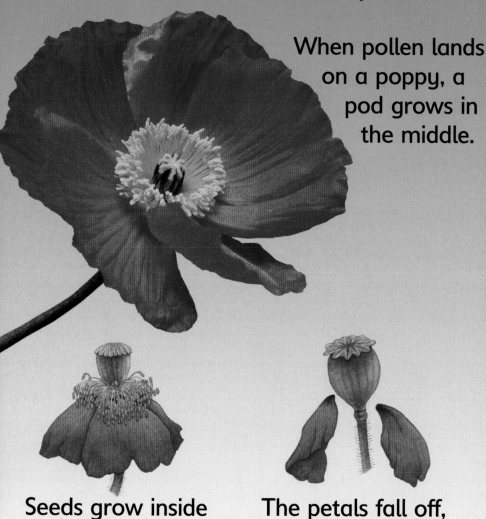

When pollen lands on a poppy, a pod grows in the middle.

Seeds grow inside the pod and the flower begins to die.

The petals fall off, leaving a pod full of seeds.

Alliums are made up of lots of tiny flowers.

Each flower becomes a tiny seed pod.

Chinese lantern seeds grow inside a hollow case.

Some caterpillars live in seed pods. When the caterpillars move, the pods seem to 'jump'.

Spreading seeds

Seeds need lots of space to grow, so they have to be scattered far apart.

Burdock seeds have sharp, spiky hooks.

They get caught on an animal's fur as it brushes past.

When the animal scratches, the seeds fall off.

Seed pod

Crane's bill plants have seed pods on thin stems.

The stems curl up and shoot the seeds out of their pods.

Dandelion seeds float on the wind like little parachutes.

When ants carry seeds into their nests to eat, some of the seeds begin to grow.

Juicy fruit

Some seeds grow inside fruit, berries and
nuts. These seeds are spread by birds
and animals.

When birds eat fruit
and berries, they
eat the seeds too.

They fly away and
the seeds are spread
in their droppings.

There are about 100 seeds inside
every blueberry.

Chipmunks eat fruit and nuts.

They take their food into their burrows to eat. The seeds are spread in their droppings.

Squirrels often bury nuts in the ground to eat later.

Then they forget about them and the seeds start to grow.

19

New plants

Some plants have special ways to make new plants.

Runner

A shoot called a runner grows out sideways from a strawberry plant.

When it touches the ground it grows roots.

A new plant grows from the roots and the runner rots away.

A small, new bulb grows on the side of a daffodil bulb.

The new bulb grows bigger and the two bulbs split apart.

Only one or two flowers grow from each daffodil bulb.

Rainforest flowers

Rainforests are warm, wet places. Trees block out sunlight, so it's dark on the ground.

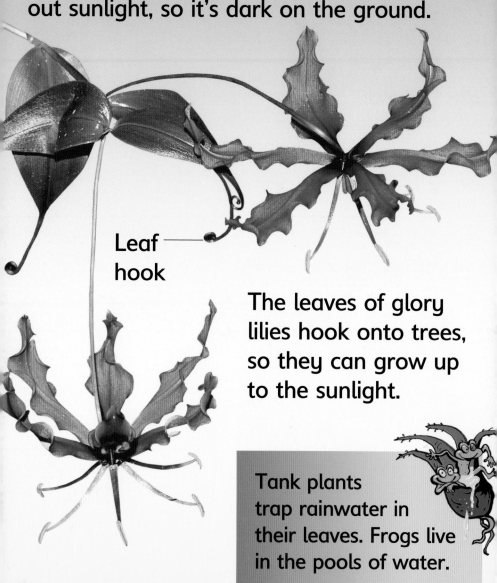

Leaf hook

The leaves of glory lilies hook onto trees, so they can grow up to the sunlight.

Tank plants trap rainwater in their leaves. Frogs live in the pools of water.

A rafflesia bud grows on the ground.

It grows as big as a cabbage.

Its five red petals start to unfold.

Rafflesia flowers are as big as the wheels on a truck and have no leaves or stems.

They smell of rotting meat to attract flies which spread their pollen.

Hot deserts

Flowers even grow in hot, dry deserts.

Some desert plants don't grow while the soil is dry, but their seeds lie in the ground.

After rain, the seeds grow quickly into flowers.

The flowers make seeds and then die.

The new seeds will grow when it rains again.

Old man cactus plants are covered in woolly hair to shade them from the sun.

When it is dry the leaves fall off an ocotillo plant.

New leaves will grow again after it has rained.

Aloe plants store water inside their thick, spiky leaves.

Water plants

Some plants grow in ponds and lakes.

Many have roots which grow on the bottom of a lake.

Some water plants have roots which float in water.

A water lily's flowers float on the surface, so that insects can reach the pollen.

Most water plants don't grow in rivers, because they would be washed away.

Water lilies have flat leaves with a waxy surface. This helps them to float.

They don't sink even if a frog sits on them.

Killer plants

Some plants catch insects and turn them into juice, which they soak up.

A fly lands in a Venus flytrap's spiky leaves.

The trap snaps shut and the fly slowly rots inside.

Sundew plants have sticky hairs which trap insects.

Pitcher plants have leaves which look like cups and are filled with water.

There is some nectar on the rim.

Ants crawl into pitcher plants to look for more nectar.

They slide into the water and drown. Then they rot.

Monkeys like to pick pitcher plants and drink the water inside.

29

Glossary of flower words

Here are some of the words in this book you might not know. This page tells you what they mean.

 seed - a hard shell with a young plant inside.

 seed pod - the part of a flower where the seeds grow.

 bulb - special underground leaves where some plants store their food.

 stamens - long tubes in the middle of a flower where pollen is made.

 pollen - a powder which plants swap with other plants to make seeds.

 nectar - a sweet juice inside flowers which animals, birds and insects drink.

 runner - a special stem which grows out sideways from some plants.

Websites to visit

If you have a computer, you can find out more about how flowers grow on the Internet. On the Usborne Quicklinks Website there are links to four fun websites.

Website 1 - Find out which parts of plants you eat.

Website 2 - Create a garden full of flowers then print the picture.

Website 3 - Play a game to make a flower grow.

Website 4 - Watch a flower bloom.

To visit these websites, go to **www.usborne-quicklinks.com** Read the Internet safety guidelines, and then type the keywords "beginners flowers".

The websites are regularly reviewed and the links in Usborne Quicklinks are updated. However, Usborne Publishing is not responsible, and does not accept liability, for the content or availability of any website other than its own. We recommend that children are supervised while on the Internet.

Index

berries, 18
bud, 10, 23
bulb, 9, 21, 30
desert, 24-25
flower, 3, 6, 7, 10-11, 12,
    13, 14, 15, 21, 22, 23,
    24, 26, 30
food, 6, 8-9, 19, 30
fruit, 18-19
leaves, 6, 7, 8, 9, 22, 23,
    25, 27, 28, 29, 30
nectar, 12-13, 29, 30
nuts, 18, 19
petals, 10, 14, 23

pod, 14, 15, 17, 30
pollen, 11, 12-13, 14, 23,
    26, 30
rainforest, 22-23
roots, 5, 6, 7, 8, 20, 26
runner, 20, 30
seed, 4-5, 11, 14-15,
    16-17, 18, 19, 24, 30
seedling, 4-5, 10
shoot, 5, 20
soil, 4, 5, 7, 24
stamens, 11, 30
stem, 6, 8, 17, 23, 30
water, 7, 8, 25, 26-27, 29

Acknowledgements

Managing editor: Fiona Watt, Managing designer: Mary Cartwright

Photo credits

The publishers are grateful to the following for permission to reproduce material:
© **Alamy:** cover (Martin Ruegner/ImageState), 5 (Bob Challinor/The Garden Picture Library), 9
(Angela Nicholson), 21 (Frank Krahmer/ImageState); © **Bruce Coleman:** 6-7 (Jorg & Petra
Wagner), 28 (Kim Taylor);© **Corbis:** 2-3 (Chris Demetriou/Frank Lane Picture Agency), 10 (Darrell
Gulin), 15 (Michelle Garrett); © **Digital Vision:** 4, 22; © **Frank Lane Picture Agency:** 29 (Mark
Moffett/Minden Pictures); © **Getty:** 1 (Bruce Heinemann), 11 (Gary Braasch), 18 (Richard H
Johnston), 31 (JH Pete Carmichael); © **Lost World Arts:** 23 (Karl Lehmann); © **Natural Visions:** 26-
27 (Heather Angel); © **NHPA:** 25 (Patrick Fagot); © **Oxford Scientific Films:** 13 (Michael Fogden);
© **Robert Harding:** 14; © **Science Photo Library:** 17 (Lynwood Chase);
© **Team Husar:** 19 (Lisa & Mike Husar). With thanks to Simon Gladding.

Vikings

Castles

How flowers grow

Knights

Living in space

Caterpillars and Butterflies

Ballet

Pirates

Egyptians

Eggs and Chicks

Romans

Dinosaurs

Tadpoles and frogs

Why do we eat?

Under the sea

Weather

Sun, Moon and stars

Farm animals

Elizabeth I

TRASH AND RECYCLING